G000075273

BECAUSE I AM INTELLIGENT

-

EASY AS P.I.E AFFIRMATIONS
Part 2

Award winning author

AMIRE BEN SALMI

aka

"Mr. Intelligent"

Published by I AM Publishing in 2019

The author asserts the moral right under the Copyright, Designs and Patents Act to be identified as the author of this work.

ISBN: 978-1-913310-20-2

DEDICATION

I want to dedicate this book to **YOU** because **YOU** are INTELLIGENT too.

DISCLAIMER

Amire Ben Salmi (the author) is a business and life coach/mentor. Nothing more and nothing less. The Author cannot, and do not, make any promises, guarantees, warrantees or representations about results other than the coaches diligent work with you. Advices are being provided "AS IS" without warranty of any kind, either express or implied, including without limitation any warranty for information, coaching, products or services provided through or in connection with this book. The advices in this book are requested at the coaching/mentoring participant's own choice and with inherent singular responsibility of the coaching/mentoring participant.

The author would like to explicitly point out that the advices that the author offer do not replace the expertise of a medical doctor or of an alternative non-medicine practitioner. Advices differ decidedly from those of a medical doctor or that of a practitioner in the non-medical area.

The author does not claim to make any diagnosis or give any promises of any sort of healing processes. The author is neither qualified nor equipped to deal with a person with pathological history, should you be in medical or psychiatric treatment due to any health issues, it is strongly advised to continue your therapy with your doctors. In case you still want to be coached/mentored by the author of this book, kindly consult your doctors before contacting the author. Whatever your decision, please do not interrupt your treatment with your doctor(s).

This book is focused on offering you a host of inspiration and resources to give you a chance to open your mind to the wonders of abundance in life for a more satisfying existence. This book will help you to learn how to loosen the control mechanisms that habitually stop us. For all other physical or mental health issues you are advised to consult professionals who are specifically trained to treat such challenges.

The author shall not be responsible for any loss or damage caused, or alleged to have been caused, directly or indirectly, by the information or ideas contained, suggested, or referenced in this book. However, if any legal relations arise in connection with this book, shall be governed by and construed in accordance with the laws of United Kingdom.

FOREWORD

My name is Lashai Ben Salmi, I am a 19-year-old **AS SEEN ON TV, RADIO & NEWSPAPERS etc.** Lashai Ben Salmi is not your average 19-year-old. She is a multi-award winning Youth Advocate, Winner of TruLittle Heros Award - Entrepreneur 2017, Speaker at Virgin Money Lounge Historical Black History Month first ever event , Guest Speaker at Mercedes Benz World, High Profile Club, YouTuber with 27K plus subscribers and over 4M plus views (KPOP Channel called *The K-Way*, An award winning author of Kidz That Dream Big, Andy Harrington ACE Coach, Former International Radio Show host, Winner of Regan Hillyer International Scholarship, a speaker, a business/personal developments mentor & coach, founder of Blossom Tree Photography & Videography (Produced content in association with Legoland Resort, Warner Bros, Harry Potter, Little Mix, Sony and Disney Pixar etc. Co-founder of A Precipice of A Dream and founder of Put The RED Card Up To bullying & My Journey - Giving Youth Several Reasons to Smile who is here to help children and youth to plant the seed for an abundance of unique opportunities via a variety of products and services to assist you to create a brighter future

Because I AM Intelligent book series is an inspirational book based on affirmations by my amazing 9-year-old brother Amire. Each time I observe my brother recite his 365 affirmations it warms my heart. I'm the eldest of five siblings and they never stop amazing me, especially Amire. He's only 6, however he's extremely intelligent. As an Andy Harrington ACE Mentor, an HSF-YLS (Harry Singha Foundation Young Leaders Summit) Lead

Coach, author and public speaker I'm constantly surrounded by amazing individuals I truly believe that children have a lot to teach, if we are willing to listen. When my brother told me, he was going to write this book I was beyond excited and told him that I'd love to write his book foreword.

Because I AM Intelligent – **365 Affirmations To Brighten Up Your Day** and this second book in the book series called Because I AM Intelligent – **Easy As P.I.E Affirmations™** is an inspirational book of affirmations, is truly an amazing read! I honestly believe that amire was the perfect person to write this book because of the fact that he has developed such a positive mind-set and attitude at such a young age and that is truly inspiring to kids of all ages.

I really believe that all kids should have a way of reminding themselves how powerful they are & that they also have the power to be, do and have whatever they desire, so long as the put their mind to! I would defiantly say that this book is very unique, in the fact that that kids will truly be able to relate to each and every affirmation.

Within this book you will find a range of fun, empowering & inspiring affirmations that will make sure that you feel empowered, inspired and filled with energy throughout the day

I truly believe that a positive and empowering mind-set can really make the biggest difference and if that can be seeded at a young age it will really allow a child to truly believe that the possibilities in life are limitless!

Like I mentioned earlier I really and truly believe that every child should have access to this book, for them to have a way of reminding themselves how amazing, powerful and unique they are.

I was felt really honoured and delighted when Amire asked me to write his forward because I cannot put into words how important I believe it is that the future generations understand their power.

Lashai Ben Salmi

U.K 19-year-old Youth Advocate, Multi-award-winning Author, Public Speaker, Andy Harrington ACE Coach, Business/Personal Development Consultant and YouTuber 27K plus subscribers

ACKNOWLEDGMENTS

Thank you so much to everyone who has helped me and my family. I would also like to say a huge thank you to Robert Vilkelis for helping me to create the system for **Easy As P.I.E Affirmations™ Part 2** because I can now run workshops and create training.

EASY AS P.I.E AFFIRMATIONS™

Without affirmations sometimes you might feel sad, lonely or bored.

I am so excited about showing you how to create affirmations that make you dance

P is for Positive. Your affirmation has to be said positively

For example

"I am happy" not "I am not sad"

I is for Inspirational. Your affirmation has to be focused towards something you want

For example

"I am smart and that feels good" not I" am not smart and I do not feel good"

E is for Energetic. Your affirmation has to make you feel like jumping up and down, dancing and you must feel it emotionally

For example

When you create affirmations always remember to SMILE, feel good inside and move your body. You can make your affirmation into a song and dance that you do in the morning and at night or anytime you want to feel happy and dance.

Step 1:

Make a list of things that make you feel sad.

For example

I am not good at maths

I am not good at football

No one likes me

Step 2:

Now make a list of affirmations that are opposite to the list that makes you feel sad.

For example

I practice maths so I can get better

I enjoy football and I get better and better every time I play

I am kind and friendly so I can make new friends that are just like me.

Step 3:

<u>Say your affirmations out loud in front of a mirror every morning when you wake up and just before you go to bed.</u> Say your affirmations over and over and over again with a big smile, move your body and have lots of fun

Affirmations can help you feel happy when you feel sad.

Well done for leaning **Easy As P.I.E Affirmations™ Part 2** you are very intelligent just like me.

ALL ABOUT YOU
Write your own affirmations ALL ABOUT YOU
☺

Today I enjoyed…

I felt happy when…

I feel happy when I play with…

I enjoy learning about…

My favourite fruit is…

My favourite vegetable…

My big dream is…

I feel safe when…

I feel loved when…

My super hero power is…

My favourite colour is…

I am good at…

I love myself because…

CREATE SOME POSITIVE AFFIRMATIONS

I Am…

I THINK…

I BELIEVE…

I KNOW…

WOULDN'T IT BE NICE IF…

I Am…

I THINK…

I BELIEVE…

I KNOW…

WOULDN'T IT BE NICE IF…

WELL DONE…

CREATE SOME LOVING AFFIRMATIONS

I Am…

I THINK…

I BELIEVE…

I KNOW…

WOULDN'T IT BE NICE IF…

I Am…

I THINK…

I BELIEVE…

I KNOW…

WOULDN'T IT BE NICE IF…

WELL DONE…

CREATE SOME FUN AFFIRMATIONS

I Am…

I THINK…

I BELIEVE…

I KNOW…

WOULDN'T IT BE NICE IF…

I Am…

I THINK…

I BELIEVE…

I KNOW…

WOULDN'T IT BE NICE IF…

WELL DONE…

MY JOURNEY OF HAVING FUN WITH MY FAMILY AND FRIENDS ....
"A PICTURE SPEAK A THOUSAND WORDS"

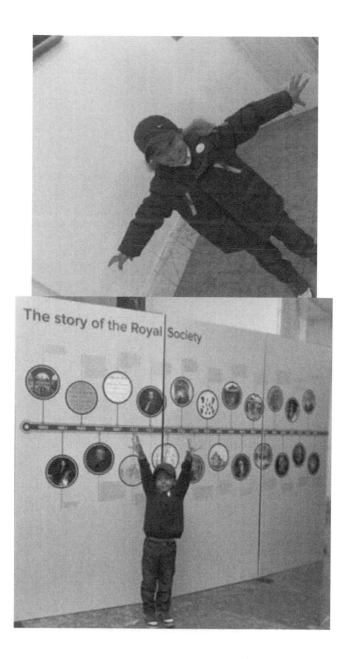

Maxine's Shout

Inspirational message to kids

'Anything is possible' for proactive 10-year-old who designs own T-shirts

365 AFFIRMATIONS TO BRIGHTEN UP YOUR DAY

**I AM
INTELLIGENT**

I AM TALENTED

I AM LOVED

I AM GIFTED

I AM SPECIAL

I AM HAPPY

I AM A BOOK WORM

I AM LIVING THE DREAM NOW

I AM AN INVESTOR

I AM LOVELY

I LOVE USING MY

IMAGINATION TO DREAM BIG

I AM A CHILD

GENIUS

I AM PEACE

I AM HOPE

I AM ME

I LOVE MY LIFE

I LOVE MYSELF

**I AM GOOD AT
SAVING**

I AM FREE

I AM PLAYFUL

I AM KIND

I AM LOVABLE

**I AM CHOOSING TO
BE PRESENT**

**I AM CHOOSING
TO BE IN THE
CHOICE**

I AM CREATIVE

I AM COOL

**I AM ALL KINDS OF
AWESOME**

**I AM GRATEFUL
FOR MY HEALTH**

I AM LEARNING

I AM A STAR

I AM A CREATOR

I AM GROWING

I AM HELPFUL

I AM FUNNY

I AM CLEVER

I AM PRESENT

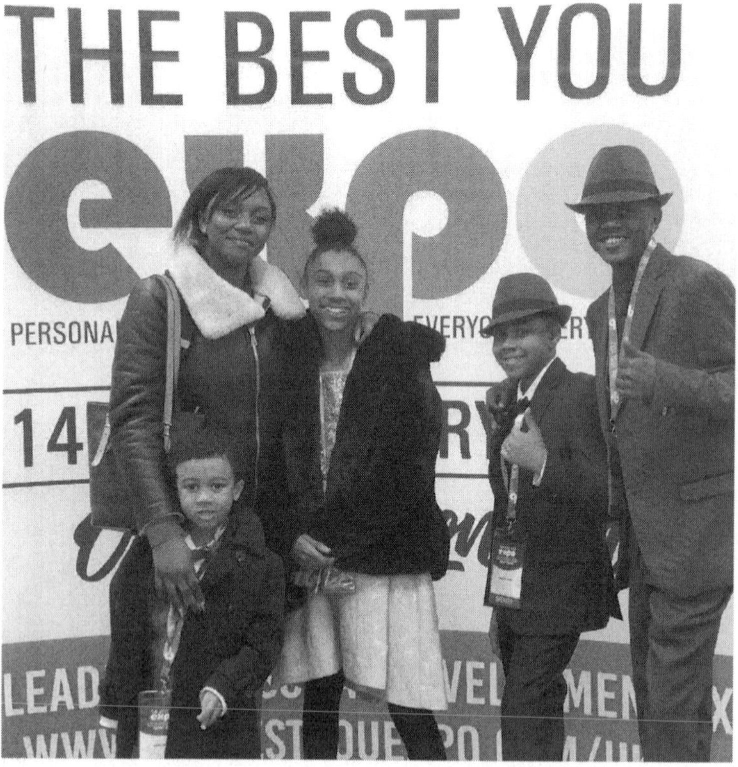
THE BEST YOU
PERSONA
14

I AM BRAVE

**I ENJOY
EXPLORING**

**I AM
ADVENTUROUS**

I AM EXCITED

**I AM DOING MY BEST
AND THAT IS GOOD
ENOUGH**

**I AM TAKING ONE
STEP AT A TIME**

**I AM A
MASTERPIECE**

**I AM PLANTING A
SEED FOR MY
FUTURE**

**I AM LOVED &
APPRECIATED**

I AM GRATEFUL

I LOVE MY FAMILY

I LOVE MY FRIENDS

**I AM A
WONDERFUL
MASTERPIECE**

I LOVE ANIMALS

I LOVE NATURE

**I LOVE TO KEEP MY
HOME TIDY WITH
MY FAMILY**

I AM THANKFUL

**I AM ABUNDANT IN
ALL AREAS OF MY
LIFE**

I AM ENJOYING MY DANCE WITH LIFE

I AM THE CAPTAIN OF MY SHIP

I AM IN ALIGNMENT

I AM CHOOSING POSITIVE ACTIONS & WORDS

I AM GRATEFUL FOR MY FAMILY & FRIENDS

I AM CHOOSING TO BE HAPPY NOW

I AM RELAXED

I AM PEACEFUL

I AM A GOOD GIVER

I AM A GOOD RECEIVER

I AM A MONEY MAGNET

I AM CHOOSING TO EMBRACE LIFE

I AM SURROUNDED BY AMAZING MENTORS

I AM CURIOUS

I AM CAPABLE

I AM A GOOD LISTENER

I AM SURROUNDED BY LOVE

I AM DOING THE BEST I CAN

I AM A LEADER

I AM A CHAMPION

**I AM LIVING THE
DREAM**

I AM ABLE

I AM THE

INSPIRATION

I AM BEAUTIFUL

I AM AN OPPORTUNITY MAGNET

I AM STRONG

I AM HONEST

I AM TRUTHFUL

I AM MAGNIFICENT

I AM CHEERFUL

I AM RESPECTFUL

I AM A GOOD FRIEND

I APPRECIATE WHAT I HAVE

I AM PRECIOUS, AND SO ARE YOU

I AM THE KEY TO THE DOOR OF OPPORTUNITIES

I HAVE POSITIVE THOUGHTS

I CAN BE, DO & HAVE WHATEVER I DESIRE

I HAVE THE POWER TO CHANGE THE WORLD WITH OTHERS

EVERYDAY IS A NEW ADVENTURE

I LOVE SMILING

I LOVE CUDDLES

I AM FORGIVING

I AM WORTHY

**I SHOW OTHERS
THAT I CARE**

**I WORK SMART, NOT
HARD**

**I AM ALWAYS OPEN TO
LEARNING NEW
THINGS**

**I AM GRATEFUL FOR
WHAT
I ACHIEVE
IN MY LIFE**

I LOVE LEARNING

I AM VALUED

I WAS BORN READY

WHEN I FALL,

I GET BACK UP

I LEARN FROM MY

MISTAKES

I AM CREATING

MORE PROSPERITY

I AM CONFIDENT

I AM SURROUNDED BY PEOPLE THAT LOVE ME

I CAN DO IT

I AM AMAZING JUST THE WAY I AM

I ALWAYS ASK QUESTIONS

I WAS BORN AMAZING

I AM THE PERSON WHO CAN LIGHT UP YOUR DAY

I ENJOY HELPING OTHERS

I LOVE TO MAKE NEW FRIENDS

I AM KIND TO MYSELF & OTHERS

I AM CREATING A MAGNIFICENT LIFE

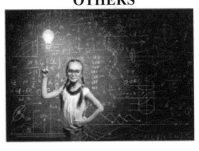

I AM GOOD AT WHATEVER I PUT MY MIND TO

I CHOOSE TO HOLD MY HEAD UP HIGH

I ALWAYS USE GOOD MANNERS

I TREAT OTHERS THE WAY I LIKE TO BE TREATED

I HAVE LOTS OF FUN EVERDAY

I FEEL FAB-U-LOUS

I AM IN CONTROL OF MY LIFE

I AM CREATING MY FUTURE NOW

I ALWAYS TRY MY BEST

I FEEL FANTASTIC

I FEEL AWESOME

I BELIEVE IN ME, YES, I DO

I AM ON TOP OF

THE WORLD

I LOVE AND

APPRECIATE THE

EARTH

I DESERVE ALL GOOD THINGS

I AM CONTENT

I LOVE TO USE MY IMAGINATION WHEN I DRAW

I LOVE TO SING FROM MY HEART

I LOVE TO DANCE LIKE NO ONE IS WATCHING

I LOVE TO USE MY IMAGINATION WHEN I PLAY

I LOVE TO SKIP

I AM EXACTLY
WHERE I NEED
TO BE

I LOVE TO RUN FAST
LIKE THE WIND

I AM PROUD TO BE
DIFFERENT

I LOVE TO EAT
HEALTHY SNACKS

TEAMWORK MAKES
THE DREAM WORK

**GOOD THINGS
HAPPEN TO ME**

**I MAKE GOOD
CHOICES**

**I VALUE MY
FRIENDSHIPS**

I AM HEALTHY

I AM WELTHY

I LOVE TO EXERCISE

EVERY LITTLE CELL IN MY BODY IS WELL

I APPRECIATE OTHERS

I AM ENERGETIC

I AM FILLED WITH COURAGE

I ALWAYS TELL THE TRUTH

I WAKE UP HAPPY IN THE MORNING

**I GO TO BED HAPPY
& ON TIME**

**I HAVE A POSITIVE
MINDSET**

**I LOVE
EVERYTHING
ABOUT MYSELF**

**I WORK WELL
IN A TEAM**

**I WORK WELL

ON MY OWN**

**THINK BIG IS A

PIECE OF CAKE**

I KNOW WHO I AM

I AM AMBITIOUS

**I WELCOME
SUCCESS
WITH OPEN ARMS**

**I AM SURROUNDED
BY ABUNDANCE**

**I WELCOME
PROPRIETY WITH
OPEN ARMS**

**MY MIND IS A
POSITIVITY MAGNET**

I AM INCREDIBLE

MY TIME IS PRECIOUS

I FOCUS ON POSITIVE CHANGE

I AM GOOD AT RECYCLING

EVERYDAY IS A NEW OPPORTUNITY

GOOD THINGS COME TO ME DAILY

MY PERSPECTIVE

**CHANGES
EVERYTHING**

I AM DESTINED FOR

GREATNESS

**I CHOOSE
TO SMILE**

**I HAVE MANY
SACRED GIFTS**

**WITH FAITH I CAN
MOVE ANYTHING**

I AM JOYFUL

**I AM DIVINE
PERFECTION**

**THANK YOU!
THANK YOU!
THANK YOU!**

I AM MY PRIORITY

**I APOLOGISE FOR
MY MISTAKES
"I AM SORRY"**

**I AM PROUD
OF MYSELF**

**STICKY SITUATIONS
CAN BE FUN**

I MAKE MISTAKES

SOMETIMES &

**WHEN I DO I
CHOOSE TO
FORGIVE MYSELF**

EACH ONE OF US IS

A BEAUTIFUL GIFT

TO THE WOLRD

I CHOOSE TO LIVE

**PEACE BEGINS
INSIDE EACH**

**I AM DESTINE TO DO
GREAT THINGS**

I AM EXPANDING

**I CHOOSE TRUST
THE PROCESS**

**IF AT FIRST I FAIL, I
SIMPLY TRY AGAIN**

**I CHOOSE TO
CREATE PEACE**

**WINNERS NEVER
QUIT & QUITERS
NEVER WIN**

I AM A PART OF

THE SOLUTION

I AM FILLED

WITH LOVE

**I AM FILLED
WITH JOY**

I AM IN FLOW

**I HAVE ENDLESS
OPPORTUNITIES**

**I KEEP TRYING
UNTIL I SUCCEED**

**READING FEEDS
MY MIND**

**I RELEASE FEAR &
WELCOME
COURAGE**

I AM THANKFUL

I AM CENTERED

I AM WISE

I TRUST MYSELF

I AM IN HARMONY

**I TREAT MYSELF
AND OTHERS
WITH KINDNESS**

I GIVE MYSELF

PERMISSION TO
SHINE

I LOVE WHEN

OTHER PEOPLE

CHOOSE TO SHINE

I LOVE WHEN
OTHER PEOPLE
CHOOSE TO BE
HAPPY

I TRUST MY
FEELINGS

I ENJOY SPENDING
TIME ON MY OWN &
WITH OTHERS

MY OPINION
MATTERS

**PEOPLE LISTEN TO
WHAT I HAVE TO SAY**

**I VALUE OTHER
PEOPLES OPINIONS**

**I AM ONE
OF A KIND**

**I AM
UNIQUE**

**I RESPECTFULLY ASK
FOR HELP
WHEN NEEDED**

**I CELEBRATE
MYSELF**

**I CELEBRATE
OTHERS**

**I CHOOSE TO
LEARN WHEN
I AM CORRECTED**

**I SHOW MY FAMILY
HOW MUCH
I LOVE THEM**

**I SHOW MY
FRIENDS HOW
MUCH I
APPRECIATE THEM**

**MY FAMILY ARE A
GIFT TO ME**

**MY FRIENDS ARE A
GIFT TO ME**

I TAKE TIME TO

**SHOW OTHERS THAT
I CARE**

I SLEEP

PEACEFULLY

I AM

COMPASSIONATE

TOWARDS ANIMALS

I AM

COMPASSIONATE

TOWARDS OTHERS

ALL IS WELL

**I AM SAFE
AND SUPPORTED**

**ALL PROBLEMS
HAVE SOLUTIONS**

**I MAKE OTHERS
FEEL VALUED**

**ALL THAT I NEED COMES
TO ME WITH EASE**

**I ALWAYS LISTEN
TO
MY HEART**

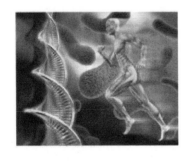

**I APPRECIATE THE
TRILLIONS OF CELLS IN
MY BODY**

**MY DREAMS
ALWAYS COME
TRUE**

I AM FRIENDLY

I CAN DO IT

**I CHOOSE TO
FOLLOW MY BLISS**

I AM GENEROUS

**I AM
PROTECTED**

**I AM GOOD AT
SOLVING
PROBLEMS**

I HAVE LOTS OF ENERGY

I CAN BECOME WHATEVER I WANT TO BE

I EMBRACE CHANGE

I MAKE FRIENDS EASILY

I AM CONTRIBUTING

I HAVE HAPPY THOUGHTS

**I FORGIVE OTHERS
FOR THEIR** MISTAKES

I AM FREE

**I AM
PERSISTENT**

**FREE WILL IS
MY BIRTHRIGHT**

I AM TRUSTWORTHY

I AM GENTLE

I AM PATIENT

LIFE IS FUN

KNOWLEDGE OPENS THE DOOR TO MY FUTURE

I LIKE BEING CHALLENGED

I AM OPTIMISTIC

I AM EXCITED ABOUT THE UNKNOWN

**RESPECT IS
IMPORTANT**

**I RECEIVE ALL THE
HELP I NEED**

**AWESOME THINGS
HAPPEN TO ME,
FAMILY & FRIENDS**

**I BELIEVE IN
MY DREAMS**

**I AM AN

ACTION TAKER**

**I APPRECIATE

EVERYONE IN
MY LIFE**

I CAN DO WHATEVER I FOCUS MY MIND ON

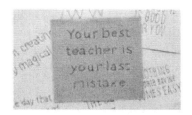

I AM A FAST LEARNER

LEARNING NEW THINGS IS FUN AND EXCITING

I CAN SEE THE BIGGER PICTURE

I HAVE POTENTIAL

I BELIEVE IN MIRACLES

**I GET BETTER
WITH PRACTICE**

**I LOVE TO WRITE
STORIES**

**I LOVE MY FAMILY
& MY HOME**

**I LOVE
BEING SMART**

**I LOVE TO EAT
VEGETABLES**

**I LOVE MY LIFE
SOOOO MUCH**

MY MIND IS FILLED WITH AMAZING THINGS

PLAY IS PRACTICE

I ACHIEVE EXTRAORDINARY RESULTS

I SEE BEAUTY EVERYWHERE I GO

MY IMAGINATION IS BEYOND AWESOME

I APPRECIATE TECHNOLOGY

**I LOVE
SCIENCE**

**I CAN CHOOSE TO
HAVE FUN ALL DAY
LONG**

I AM A SUPER HERO

I LIKE TO DISCOVER

NEW PLACES

**I LOVE LEARNING
EVERYDAY**

I LOVE MATHS

**I AM EXCELLENT
AT ENGLISH**

**I AM EXCELLENT
AT SCIENCE**

**I AM EXCELLENT
AT HISTORY**

**I AM EXCELLENT
AT GEOGRAPHY**

**I AM EXCELLENT
AT SPORTS**

**I AM EXCELLENT
AT ART**

**MY IMAGINATION
MAKES LIFE FUN**

I LOVE MUSIC

**I ENJOY DOING MY
HOMEWORK**

**I JUMP FOR JOY IN
LIFE**

I RUN FREE WITH

I CHOOSE TO FOCUS

MY FRIENDS

ON MY DREAMS

I LOVE TO LEARN DIFFERENT LANGUAGES

I CHOOSE TO TOUCH THE WORLD WITH LOVE, PEACE AND KINDNESS

READING IS THE DIFFERENCE THAT MAKES THE DIFFERENCE

I APPRECIATE NATURE, IT IS BEAUTIFUL

IT FEELS GOOD TO GIVE

I AM INTELLIGENT & MIGHTY

**FAMILIES THAT
PLAY TOGETHER,
STAY TOGETHER**

**I AM WORKING ON MY
FUTURE**

**I CAN SEE BEAUTY
THROUGH MY
WINDOW**

**I BELIEVE THAT
SOMETHING AWESOME
IS ABOUT TO HAPPEN**

**FAMILY IS THE
CENTER OF MY
WOLRD**

**I BELIEVE IN
MYSELF, BECAUSE I
HAVE THE POWER TO
ACHIEVE**

I AM A BEST SELLING AUTHOR

I AM ON TOP OF THE WORLD

THERE IS ALWAYS FUN THINGS TO DO OUTSIDE

I CAN BECOME A DRUMMER WHEN I USE MY IMAGINATION

I ENJOY TIME WITH FRIENDS IN NATURE

I LEARN BEST WHEN I'M HAPPY

**I ENJOY
SAVING MONEY**

I AM STRONG

I SAY "MAY I BE

EXCUSED"

WHEN I FINISH

EATING

I ASK BEFORE I

TOUCH SOMEONE

ELSES BELONGINGS

**I LOVE KNOWING
THAT ALL IS WELL**

**I ENJOY HAVING FUN
LEARNING WITH MY
FRIENDS**

**I ENJOY TAKING
CARE OF OUR
ENVIRONMENT**

**I AM A UNIQUE
PIECE TO THE
PUZZLE**

**I ONLY NEED TO
TAKE ONE STEP AT
A TIME**

**THERE IS ALWAYS
SPACE FOR
IMPROVEMENT**

**I MAKE SPACE FOR
GROWTH**

**I CHOOSE TO SOAR
LIKE AN EGALE**

**I WELCOME
FEEDBACK**

**I LIKE TO ASK
QUESTIONS**

I LOVE MY BODY

I LOVE TO LAUGH

SHIFT HAPPENS

BE IN THE CHOICE

I ENCOURAGE OTHERS TO SHINE

IT IS POSSIBLE, ONE SEED AT A TIME

I CHOOSE TO BELIEVE THAT THE IMPOSSIBLE IS POSSIBLE

THOUGHTS BECOME THINGS

TOGETHER ANYTHING IS POSSIBLE

I HAVE A DREAM

I CAN CHANGE THE WORLD ONE THOUGHT AT A TIME

I AM A GOOD ROLE MODEL

ALL OF LIFE SUPPORTS ME

CREATIVITY IS MY NATURAL STATE

I CHOOSE TO BE THE CHANGE I WANT TO SEE IN THE WORLD

I AM FORTUNATE

**I AM
ENERGY**

**I LOVE BEING A
MILLIONAIRE**

I AM UNSTOPPABLE

**I AM
CHARITABLE**

**I AM
FEEDING MY MIND**

**I AM A
PHILANTHROPIST**

**I AM
INFINITE**

**I AM
IMMEASURABLE**

**I AM

OUTSTANDING**

**I AM WAKING UP

TO

MY DREAMS
& ASPIRATIONS**

**I AM A
GO GETTER**

**WELL DONE FOR READING THE
365 AFFIRMATIONS
PLEASE LEAVE A REVIEW FOR THE
BOOK ON AMAZON**

YOU ARE AWESOME

**NOW MY FAMILY ARE GOING TO SHARE SOME
BONOUS INFORMATION WITH YOU**

CREATE YOUR OWN AFFIRMATIONS

Did you know that affirmations are simply belief statements? So you can choose to have a negative belief or a positive belief about yourself and others.

To create your own positive affirmation simply choose one negative thought and then simply come up with a positive one to counteract the negative one. For example, "I never get things right." Then your new belief could be "There's no such thing as failure, only feedback." **Make your affirmations short so they're easier for you to remember.**

1) _____
2) _____
3) _____
4) _____
5) _____
6) _____
7) _____
8) _____
9) _____
10) _____

ABOUT THE AUTHOR

AMIRE BEN SALMI

So much for the so called saying "You're too young"

Amire Ben Salmi is not your average 6yr old. Amire Ben Salmi aka Mr Because I AM Intelligent is a 6yr old award winning author of Because I AM Intelligent - 365 Affirmations To Brighten Up Your Day.

Amire was a guest speaker at The Beat You Expo: https://youtu.be/Fz9mErJC8rA where there were 15,000 attendees. Amire is the founder of I AM Publishing House. Amire hosts his signature program called Because I AM Intelligent - Easy As P.I.E Affirmations held at Virgin Money Haymarket Lounge. Amire has participated in campaigns for Sainsburys, Legoland, Warner Bros and Sony to name a few.

Amires signature program is Easy-As-P.I.E Affirmations™

Amire is founder of Because I AM Intelligent who is here to help you to plant the seed toward having fun learning during childhood, Positive Affirmations, Fun and Creativity in abundance via a variety of products such as a book with a matching colour car and 52 affirmation cards to assist you to create a brighter future.

Amire enjoys having fun learning with affirmations and he believes that words are very powerful.

The question is when will you choose to affirm your life?

Amire is the youngest of five siblings:
18YR OLD LASHAI, 14YR OLD TRAY-SEAN, 11YR OLD YASMINE and 9YR OLD PAOLO
Together they are known as

"The Fantastic FIVE"

DID YOU KNOW?

Did YOU know that we all develop our belief systems about ourselves and the world around us from our environment?

Our family and friends, role models, television, magazines and advertising can either be nurturing or damaging. It is important that we, our families and our friends learn to take control of our belief systems and the younger that we do, the easier it is. It can be as simple as affirming the positive beliefs that we would like to grow up with. Negative beliefs can impact our lives greatly and can be hard to shift as we grow older. Affirmations are a powerful and holistic way of building positive mind and happier children and will go onto help them through their lives._This will also nurture their authentic self and help them to enjoy the magic of childhood.

Put simply, Because I Am Intelligent - 365 Affirmations To Brighten Up Your Day aims to affirm to one's self positive words that are absorbed by the mind to create your belief system. Once affirmations are learned, they work by coming to mind when that belief is challenged. For example if your affirmation is "I am wonderful just the way I am", and you are told you are stupid, the affirmation will come to mind to remind you of your belief.

Instead, you will think, "I'm not stupid, I am wonderful!" Without a positive belief, you may take on the one you just heard and start to believe that you are stupid. The more an affirmation is repeated, positive or negative, the stronger it becomes.

119

ABOUT THE BEN SALMI FAMILY

BYA Mother of The Year Award Winner Sabrina Ben Salmi BSc is a proud mother of 5 Entrepreneurial children aged 5yrs old to 18yrs old who she referees to as her Fantastic 5.

SABRINA BEN SALMI BSc
'THE GLOBAL CONNECTOR'

AS SEEN ON TV, RADIO, NEWSPAPERS etc. Multi award winner and Mother of The Year Award Winner.

Sabrina Ben Salmi BSc is also an Award Winning author who went from being lone parent mother of two and faced with a wealth of adversities to becoming a lone parent coach filled with a dream and a burning desire to enrich the lives of lone parent families both locally and globally. To date Sabrina she is now married and a proud mother of 5 entrepreneurial children who are also multi award winners and award winning authors aged 5yrs to 18yrs old who she refers to as her Fantastic 5 (Lashai 18, Tray-Sean 13, Yasmine 11, Paolo 9 and Amire 5).

Sabrina chose to turn her adversities into empowerment in the hope of inspiring her dependents and her global clients both current and future to allow themselves to take steps towards building their dreams so that they can have fun learning. She went on a journey of self-discovery so that she could learn to turn LEMONS INTO LEMONADE.

Sabrina has been assisting individuals and businesses since 2006 as a professional and business transformation consultant, empowering them to achieve their goals, to be successful, to feel more connected, confident, fulfilled, acknowledged and loved. In other words, she ignites their burning desire to start living the life they've always dreamt of. Sabrina is passionate about the intricacies of the mind, our surrounding environment, being fully alive, dancing with the universe and paying it forward.

Sabrina's background is in Computer Science, Sabrina is co-foundering director of Harris Invictus Academy (OfSted Outstanding Secondary School). Sabrina is founder of The Mobile Single Parents Project™, Dreaming Big Together™, MindSet-ReSet Now™, The Conscious Entrepreneur Blueprint™, Mamas Secret Recipe™ & Shift Happens™ transformational Programs. It is said that Sabrina is the mentor of many successful and famous individuals and responsible local and global personal and professional connections that have gone on to influence business and individuals across the globe.

Sabrina is also a qualified Personal Performance Coach, Access Consciousness Practitioner, Master Results Coach, and Master Practitioner in Neuro-Linguistic Programming (NLP), Advanced Subconscious Reprogramming and Hypnotherapy. Sabrina Ben Salmi BSc continues to immerse herself in an abundance of knowledge through a variety mediums. Sabrina and her family believe in the importance of investing in their personal development and encourage you to do so too. Regan Hillyer & Juan Barahona are currently the Ben Salmi family mentors.

Sabrina is a Make Your Mark Ambassador, PRECIOUS AWARD finalist, British Library case study; and has attracted the attention of both National and International media across TV, Newspapers and radio etc for instance BBC London News, BBC, BBC Radio, Colourful Radio, Channel 4 documentaries (The Secret Millionaire etc).

She is also a fellow of the School of Social Entrepreneurs (SSE), A Glimmer of Hope award winner, Urban Futures award winner, an Unltd Award winner and nominated to carry the Olympic Torch 2012.

Sabrina is involved in a variety of diverse projects in a variety of industries both locally and globally ranging from renewable energy, oil to education and personal development. She has a burning desire to inspire and empower others to attain their deepest desires.

Sabrina is extremely passionate about children and youth empowerment and is responsible for the majority of the new stream of child/youth entrepreneurs/authors that are newly visible and coming into the personal development world.

"It's about time that we stop giving our children indefinite time to remain on the streets and leaving their future to chance. Instead empower them to plant the seed for a brighter tomorrow"

Sabrina and her family have a family mantra and an anthem that they live by.

My book: Lone Parenthood: Essential Tips on How to Create the Life You Deserve

A link to my book:

http://www.fast-print.net/bookshop/897/lone-parenthood-essential-tips-on-how-to-create-the-life-you-deserve

https://www.amazon.co.uk/dp/178035066X/ref=cm_sw_r_cp_api_i_tA15AbZ1T0Y31
Sabrina specialises in:
Personal/professional development and YOUTH ENTREPRENEURSHIP. Sabrina has two signature programs called Mamas Secret Recipe™, The Conscious Entrepreneur Blueprint™ & 21 Day Shift Happens™. Sabrina also specialises in Professional Connections, Corporate Engagement, Workshops and Public Speaking

You can contact Sabrina Ben Salmi BSc via the details below:

Email: sabrinabensalmi@me.com

Sabrina's book: Lone Parenthood: Essential Tips on How to Create the Life You Deserve
https://www.amazon.co.uk/dp/178035066X/ref=cm_sw_r_cp_api_i_tA15AbZ1T0Y31

AS SEEN OF TV & NEWSPAPERS Mohamed Ben Salmi is the father and step-father of The Fantastic Five. Mohamed loves sports, speaks multiple languages and is a store manager with a passion for travel.

AS SEEN OF TV, RADIO & NEWSPAPERS etc. (BBC Korea:

https://www.facebook.com/818434098337843/posts/12210 18028079446?sfns=mo) etc. Lashai Ben Salmi aka DREAMPRENEUR is not your average 18yr old.

She is a multi-award winning Youth Advocate, Property Mentor & Investor, Presented award for TruLittle Heros Award 2018, Social Media Content Creator for The Korean Cultural Centre, Winner of TruLittle Heros Award - Entrepreneur 2017 and Speaker at Virgin Money Lounge Historical Black History Month first ever event.

Lashai is founder of Stepping Stones Publishing House.

Lashai hosts her signature program called Stepping Stones at Virgin Money Lounge

The Beat You Expo (15,000 attendees), Mentioned in Carolyn A Brent book called: Across All Ages DEEP BEAUTY Lashai is one of 14 VIP names mentioned which is in the congress library in Washington DC.

Guest Speaker at Mercedes Benz World 10th April 2018, High Profile Club, YouTuber with 26K plus subscribers and over 4M plus views (Korean Channel), An award winning author of Kidz That Dream Big, Andy Harrington ACE Coach, Former International Radio Show host, Winner of Regan Hillyer International Scholarship, a speaker. Lashai is a Regan Hillyer International Team Member, a business/personal developments Consultant.

Founder of Blossom Tree Photography & Videography Produced content in association with Legoland Resort, Harry Potter, Little Mix and Disney Pixar, Sony, Warner Brothers & Universal etc.

Co-founder of A Precipice of A Dream and founder of Put The RED Card Up To bullying & My Journey - Giving Youth Several Reasons to Smile who is here to help children and youth to plant the seed for an abundance of unique opportunities via a variety of products and services to assist you to create a brighter future

Lashai has been mentored by some of the leading name within the personal development world Regan Hillyer, Andy Harrington, Cheryl Chapman, Harry Singha, Ralph Plumb, Sammy Blindell to name a few. Lashai has shared the stage with the likes of the late Dr. Miles Monrune, Dr. John Demartini, Andy Harrington, Robert G Allen and Ralph Plumb to name a few.

If you are looking for an inspiring, wise, talented, refreshing and powerful speaker then 18yr old Lashai Ben Salmi is guaranteed to make a big impact at your event. Lashai has been a part of the personal development world since the age of 11yrs.

Lashai has a burning desire to transform lives with her stage presence, knowledge and wisdom! Lashai's signature topics include: Congruency, Alignment, Self-Belief, YouTube, Social Media, Connection, Inspiration and Motivation.

Lashai's signature program: The Stepping Stone's Formula™ & YouSmart - How to Work Smart, Not Hard On YouTube™

Lashai's Books:

1. Kidz That Dream Big: Dreams Do Come True
https://www.amazon.co.uk/dp/1912547066/ref=cm_sw_r_cp_api_mwbUAbS8BTQHE

2. Kidz That Dream Big!...
https://www.amazon.co.uk/dp/1909039322/ref=cm_sw_r_cp_api_i_eMZKCbNSJ3JDX

3. KIDZ THAT DREAM BIG!: The Stepping Stones Formula™
https://www.amazon.co.uk/dp/B07NJ8YLHM/ref=cm_sw_r_cp_api_i_RMZKCbG7CXZBJ

Facebook page: Kidz That Dream Big:
https://www.facebook.com/Kidz-that-Dream-BIG-154694734627138/

AS SEEN OF TV, RADIO & NEWSPAPERS etc
Tray-Sean Ben Salmi aka I'm That KID is not your average 14yr old. Tray-Sean Ben Salmi is a 14yr old Amazon #1 Best Seller & Award-Winning Author, Stock & Shares Trader, Property Mentor & Investor, Award winning Public Speaker (Virgin, The Beat You Expo 15,000 attendees) and Child Advocate. Tray-Sean has recently signed a contract with FirstPoint USA 🇺🇸 for an opportunity to go to America for a full academic and sports scholarship

Child Genius 2017 top 20 smartest children in the UK as a result Tray-Sean was 1 out of 34 boys to be invited to sit papers at the prestigious Eton College.

Tray-Sean is founder of Influencer Publishing House.

Tray-Sean hosts his signature program called I'm That KID at Virgin Money Lounge

Tray-Sean is an award winning author of Kidz That Dream Big, Former Radio Show host, Regan Hillyer International Be Your Brand Fellow, Author of 10 Seconds To Child Genius, Winner of TruLittle Heros Award - Academic, Business/Personal developments mentor & coach.

Tray-Sean participated in brand campaigns for Sainsburys, Legoland, Warner Bros, Sony and Official Judges for Made For Mums Toy Awards to name a few.

Tray-Sean is founder of I'm That KID covers:

- I'm That KID - Bridging The Gap Between Fathers & Sons™

- I'm That KID – Creating A Vision Board for My Future™

- I'm That KID – Taking The Stage™

- I'm That KID - Inspiring My Community To Pay It Forward™

- I'm That KID - There's A Book Inside ME™

- I'm That KID - Families That Play Together Stay Together™

- I'm That KID - Empowering You To Step Into Your POWER™

- I'm That KID - BEING The Change That I Desires To See In The World™

10 Seconds To Child Genius is a book series co-founded by Tray-Sean Ben Salmi & Philip Chan. This book series aims to help children and young people to plant the seed today to create a brighter future tomorrow.

Q : How do you know what you DON'T KNOW?
A : When someone point out the obvious which you have overlooked!

There is a mis-conception that only a limited amount of people can be a 'Child Genius'. In this book Tray-Sean Ben Salmi show you this 'myth' is not true.

JUST KNOW THAT YOU CAN HELP YOUR CHILD TO DISCOVER THEIR GENIUS WITHIN.

Tray-Sean's signature program: I'M That KID Blueprint™

Tray-Sean's Books:

1. 10 Seconds To Child Genius
https://www.amazon.co.uk/dp/099286948X/ref=cm_sw_r_cp_api_uxbUAbPH5C3K1

2. I'm That KID: Empowering You to Step Into Your Power
https://www.amazon.co.uk/dp/B07PXFS7TY/ref=cm_sw_r_cp_api_i_TGZKCb0188EG1

3. 10 Seconds To Child Genius: The Road To Child Genius
https://www.amazon.co.uk/dp/B07PXBS2MQ/ref=cm_sw_r_cp_api_i_CIZKCbDFPKRF7

4. 10 Seconds To Child Genius: From Eton Road To Eton College
https://www.amazon.co.uk/dp/B07P9K469N/ref=cm_sw_r_cp_api_i_rJZKCb951S2FV

5. Kidz That Dream Big!...
https://www.amazon.co.uk/dp/1909039322/ref=cm_sw_r_cp_api_i_-JZKCbYJFFCAD

6. Kidz That Dream Big: Dreams Do Come True
https://www.amazon.co.uk/dp/1912547066/ref=cm_sw_r_cp_api_i_9KZKCbD0XTRYA

7. Property Problem Solver: Has Your Property Become A Pain In Your Life?
https://www.amazon.co.uk/dp/B07Q7WX3MY/ref=cm_sw_r_cp_api_i_1cGOCb2XT7BEP

Facebook page: 10 Seconds To Child Genius:
https://m.facebook.com/10secondstochildgenius/

AS SEEN OF TV, RADIO & NEWSPAPERS etc

Yasmine Ben Salmi is not your average 12yr old.

Yasmine Ben Salmi aka LovePreneur is an 11yr award winning author of The Choice is Your - 10 Keys Principles To Create A Happier Lifestyle and Winner of TruLittle Heros Award - Creative 2017.

Guest Speaker at Best You Expo (15,000 attendees) and Former International Radio Show Host.

Yasmine is the founder of The Choice Is Yours Publishing House.

Yasmine hosts her signature program called The Choice Is Yours - Your Thinking C.A.P For Living & Loving Life at Virgin Money Lounge

Yasmine participated in campaigns for Sainsburys, Legoland, Warner Bros, Sony and Made For Mums to name a few.

Yasmine's signature program: Your Thinking C.A.P For Living & Loving Life™

Yasmine is founder of Dog Walking Service "Woof-Woof your dog is here".

Yasmine was nominated for a R.E.E.B.A Award 2017, Winner of Radio Works Authors Awards 2017 and nominated for National Diversity Award 2017.

Yasmine is also the founder of Mother and Daughter Connect Collection and founder of Lovepreneure.

Yasmine dreams to be the change that she desires to see in the world and inspire others to be in the choice as often as possible.

The question is when will you start living life on your terms?

Books:

1.   The Choice Is Yours: 10 Key Principles to Create a Happier Lifestyle
https://www.amazon.co.uk/dp/1912547082/ref=cm_sw_r_cp_api_JbaUAbR7K3MNS

2.   The Choice Is Yours: Your Thinking C.A.P For Living & Loving

https://www.amazon.co.uk/dp/1912999048/ref=cm_sw_r_cp_api_i_5NZKCb3D9TGNY

Facebook   page: Lovepreneure: https://m.facebook.com/YasmineBenSalmiakaLovePrenur/

AS SEEN OF TV, RADIO & NEWSPAPERS etc 10yr old Paolo Ben Salmi aka Pint Size Adventurer is not is not your average 9yr old.

Paolo is Water-to-Go's youngest ever ambassador!
https://www.watertogo.eu/paolobensalmi

blog about Water-to-Go and Paolo:
https://www.watertogo.eu/blog/meet-paolo-water-to-gos-youngest-ever-ambassador/

Paolo is the founder of Adventurous Publishing House.

Paolo hosts her signature program called Pint Size Adventurer - The Abundant Adventure Creator at Virgin Money Lounge

Paolo Ben Salmi is an award winning author of Pint Size Adventurer - 10 Keys Principles To Get Your KIDS off their iPads & Into The Wild.

Paolo is an Award Winning Public Speaker (who has spoken at eleventh such as Mercedes Benz World and Virgin etc).

Paolo has participated in brand campaigns for Sainsburys, Legoland, Warner Bros, Sony and Made For Mums to name a few.

Paolos signature program is called The Abundant Adventure Inventor™

TruLittle Heros Award - U12 Entreprenur 2017, Guest Speaker at The Beat You Expo (15,000 attendees)

Mercedes Benz World 10th April, Official Judge for Made For Mums Toy Awards 2018 via Team Trouble, Former International Radio Show host

2017 Paolo made history by being the youngest to interview Dr John Demartini: https://www.facebook.com/350400542063654/videos/363072487463126/

Personal developments coach and founder of Pint Size Adventurer who is here to help you to plant the seed toward self discovery, exploration of the internal and external world and adventurer in abundance via a variety of products and services to assist you to create a brighter future

Paolo desires to encourage as many children as possible to go on adventures both internally and externally to activate their natural curiosity.

The question is are you watching the movie, in the movie or directing the movie?

Books:

1. Pint Size Adventurer: 10 Key Principles To Get Your KIDS off Their iPads & Into The Wild
https://www.amazon.co.uk/dp/1912547031/ref=cm_sw_r _cp_api_iwXXAbMZRM7QA

2. Pint Sized Adventurer: The Abundant Adventure Creator
https://www.amazon.co.uk/dp/1912999056/ref=cm_sw_r _cp_api_i_YOZKCbXBNE59T

Facebook page: Pint Size Adventurer:
https://m.facebook.com/paolobensalmiakapintsizeadvent urer/

AS SEEN OF TV, RADIO & NEWSPAPERS etc Amire Ben Salmi is not your average 6yr old.

Amire Ben Salmi aka Mr Because I AM Intelligent is a 6yr old award-winning author of Because I AM Intelligent - 365 Affirmations To Brighten Up Your Day. Amire was a guest Speaker at The Beat You Expo (15,000 attendees).

Amire is the founder of I AM Publishing House

Amire hosts his signature program called Because I AM Intelligent - Easy As P.I.E Affirmations at Virgin Money Lounge. Amire has participated in campaigns for Sainsburys, Legoland, Warner Bros and Sony to name a few.

Amires signature program is Easy-As-P.I.E Affirmations™

Amire is founder of Because I AM Intelligent who is here to help you to plant the seed toward having fun learning during childhood, Positive Affirmations, Fun and Creativity in abundance via a variety of products such as a book with a matching colour car and 52 affirmation cards to assist you to create a brighter future.

Amire enjoys having fun learning with affirmations and he believes that words are very powerful.

The question is when will you choose to affirm your life? Books:

3.   Because I AM Intelligent 365 Affirmations To Brighten Up Your Day
https://www.amazon.co.uk/dp/1912547023/ref=cm_sw_r _cp_api_gcaUAb6A5W5SJ

4.   Because I AM Intelligent: Easy As P.I.E Affirmations
https://www.amazon.co.uk/dp/1912999005/ref=cm_sw_r _cp_api_i_uPZKCb14F8W6W

Facebook page: Because I AM Intelligent:
https://m.facebook.com/BecauseIAMIntelligent/

OUR FAMILY BELIEFS & OUR FAMILY ANTHEM
We believe that there is no such thing as failure only
feedback.
We also believe that the journey of one-thousand miles
begins with a single step in the right direction
Family Anthem:
If you want to be somebody,
If you want to go somewhere,
You better wake up and PAY ATTENTION
I'm ready to be somebody,
I'm ready to go somewhere,
I'm ready to wake up and PAY ATTENTION!

The question is ARE YOU?

OUR NAN MARY PAUL

Mary Paul is the founder of MARY PAUL. She produces bespoke art and furniture for the high-end market. Author and Award-winning speaker Mary Paul is former radio show host, author and the founder of MARY PAUL. Mary became a single parent and her child needed a lot of care due to childhood illnesses.

Mary launched a community project with to get the community engaged and her furniture was perturbed in the newspaper with the Queen of Jordan.

Mary has exhibited her furniture in exhibitions such as Hidden Aart, 100% Design and Top Draw to name a few.

Mary has many dreams and desires to live the legacy and then leave a legacy for generations to come.

The inspiration behind MARY PAUL was to end, once and for all, what she saw as "the dubious concept of so-called single parenthood".

Mary desired to make her mark and felt that expressing herself through the medium of art. Be that furniture, paintings, home staging, personal stylist that was the difference that made the difference for her and her clients.

Mary is a family woman and is now a proud mother of one daughter and 5 grandchildren.

Mary believes that self-care is the core essence of success.

She desires to touch the hearts of others and inspire them to enhance their personal style, their home and their garden.

The question is when will you choose to pour into your own life, so much so that you can share with others as your cup runneth over?

Book:
The Carers Blueprint: 10 Key Principles To Improve The Quality of Life For The Person You Care For
https://www.amazon.co.uk/dp/1912999099/ref=cm_sw_r_cp_api_i_sfsPCb6CK9OPC

Facebook Page:

https://www.facebook.com/281125102563358/posts/296
695597672975?sfns=mo

HOW AMIRE CREATED HIS BRAND

Amire did not speak at all when he was on stage with his family for their Dreaming Big Together events back in 2017. Until one day when Amire asked his mum a question.

Amire "Mummy, do you know why I do not talk when I go on stage?"

Mum "No son, please tell me"

Amire "Because I don't have a brand like my brothers and sisters"

Mum "Oh wow Amire, thank you for sharing. Do you know what a brand is?"

Amire "Yes, it's your message to the world"

Mum "Oh wow, you are very smart Amire. What would you like to call your brand?"

Amire "Because I AM Intelligent"

Mum "Oh wow! Amire you are beyond amazing. I love the name of your new brand. Will you go on stage to speak now?"

Amire "Yes mum"

The next time Amire attended an event he went on stage and said

Amire "Hello my name is Amire Ben Salmi and I am 4yrs old and my brand is called Because I AM Intelligent. I sell a book, t-shirts and cars"

So, you see from a simple conversation a brand is born and to date Amire enjoys speaking to people about his brand and products.

THE AWESOME THING IS, NOW THAT YOU KNOW THAT AMIRE DID IT. THAT MEANS YOU CAN TOO.

10 FACTS ABOUT YOUR BRAIN

FACT ONE:
There are always 4 Stages of Learning

Stage One – UNCONSCIOUS INCOMPETENCE

This is when you start doing something new by 'Trial and Error' and hoping it will work. Does it? Hmm!

Stage Two – CONSCIOUS INCOMPETENCE

This is the 'MAKE or BREAK' stage and often 95% people will give up at this stage if they don't get success quickly and as a consequence, they will NEVER discover their real potential.
So it is vital to get a Mentor, Coach or an Instructor.

For example, if you want to learn to drive a car then book a serious course of lessons with a Qualified Driving Instructor.

Stage Three – CONSCIOUS COMPETENCE

Yes! You can do it.
Like after a number of lessons you know how to drive a car, but you still need to think of everything you are doing to drive the car safely!

Stage Four: UNCONSCIOUS COMPETENCE

You have Mastered the skill because you had so much practice and can do it without thinking about it.

FACT TWO:
We all have a Preferred Learning Style
known as V.A.K.

V - VISUAL (We learn by Reading or Looking at the information)

A - AUDITORY (We learn by Listening or Talking)

K - KINESTHETICS (We learn by Doing and being Active)

To increase our skills factor, ideally, we want to develop over time all three styles V, A and K.

FACT THREE:
We actually have five Types of W.I.R.E.S. Memory.

W - WORKING MEMORY (Short Term Memory)

I - IMPLICIT MEMORY (Or sometimes called 'The Muscle' memory. Once you have learned to do something, like how to use a new computer software etc.)

R - REMOTE (This is your lifetime accumulation of skills and knowledge and seems to diminish with age if you don't use it. "USE IT or LOSE IT")

E - EPISODIC (This is when you have a memory of a specific experience or an event.)

S - SEMANTIC (This is when certain words and symbols are special to the individual.)

FACT FOUR:
Learn to Search and Recognize Patterns that enhance Brain development.

FACT FIVE:
Your ability to learn is 'State' dependent
So have a High Expectation - when you learn you will succeed.

FACT SIX:
Emotions and Learning are closely linked.

Watch what you are saying to yourself when learning.
Have a high expectation of yourself.

Don't say:
"I will never be able to learn all these things"

Instead, say something like:

"Everything I learn I will remember at the right time to use it."

FACT SEVEN:
We all have 'DUAL' Daily Learning cycles

The two cycles are:
"Low to high energy" and "Relaxation to Tension" Cycle.
So be aware of your best time for learning, especially for test revision.

FACT EIGHT:
Our brain modal switches over roughly every 90 minutes.

Generally speaking, our left brain is more efficient for verbal skills and our right brain for spatial skills.

FACT NINE:
Our Learning and Physical performance is affected by our biological rhythms throughout the day.

Even our breathing has cycles.
Overall, short term memory is best in the morning and not so effective in the afternoon.
Whilst our long-term memory is better in the afternoon.

FACT TEN:
Your brain needs Deep Relaxing sleep.

This allows time for your brain to process all the things you have learned.
Getting into a REM sleep (Dreaming) has been found by researchers to be very important for learning.

KEEP IN TOUCH WITH 6yr old VIA SOCIAL MEDIA:

YouTube: Amire Ben Salmi
Instagram: Authoramirebensalmi
Twitter: @AmireBenSalmi
Facebook: Because I AM Intelligent

Please do not hesitate to get in touch:
becauseiamintelligent@yahoo.com or
info@iampublishingnow.com

PLEASE LEAVE A REVIEW FOR THIS BOOK ON AMAZON, THANK YOU IN ADVANCE

SURPRISE BONUS

Luster's PRODUCTS INC.

SABRINA BEN SALMI AKA MUM

Amire has been having so much fun learning. Recently Amire and his siblings have been expanding their awareness by learning about Emotional Intelligence. As a mother I feel that it is extremely important for children to learn key life skills as young as possible, and Emotional Intelligence is a life skill that is the difference that makes the difference. Please allow me to share some of what we learned with you.

As a family when we have learned to acknowledge our emotions not matter what the emotion is.

162

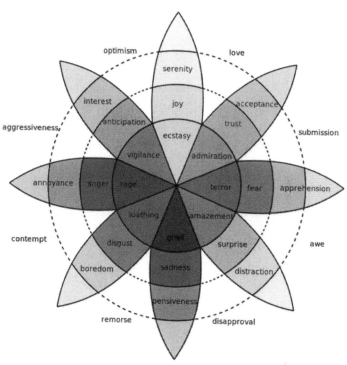

Once we acknowledge the emotion next, we differentiate and analyse the emotion. It is extremely important that we learn to accept and appreciate the emotion as there's a reason why the emotions show up, after all our emotions are merely our internal guidance system. So, it would serve you to take a moment to reflect on your emotions and its origins and what it came to teach you. It is vital that you do not suppress your emotions, it'd serve your to address and express your emotion. Being aware of other people's emotions is just as important as being aware of your own emotions.

163

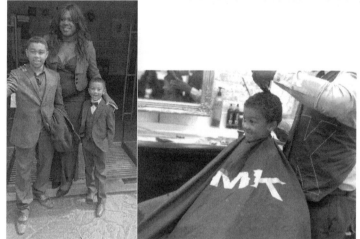